PIANO
SOLO

THE MONSTERS COLLECTION

SELECTIONS FROM *Disney* · PIXAR

MONSTERS, INC. and MONSTERS UNIVERSITY

MONSTERS, INC.

MONSTERS UNIVERSITY

WALT DISNEY MUSIC COMPANY
WONDERLAND MUSIC COMPANY, INC.

Disney and Disney/Pixar characters and artwork © Disney Enterprises, Inc.

ISBN 978-1-4803-5458-6

DISTRIBUTED BY

HAL•LEONARD®
CORPORATION
7777 W. BLUEMOUND RD. P.O. BOX 13819 MILWAUKEE, WI 53213

In Australia Contact:
Hal Leonard Australia Pty. Ltd.
4 Lentara Court
Cheltenham, Victoria, 3192 Australia
Email: ausadmin@halleonard.com.au

Visit Hal Leonard Online at
www.halleonard.com

MONSTERS, INC.

SCARE
GAMES

MONSTERS
UNIVERSITY

IF I DIDN'T HAVE YOU

Music and Lyrics by
RANDY NEWMAN

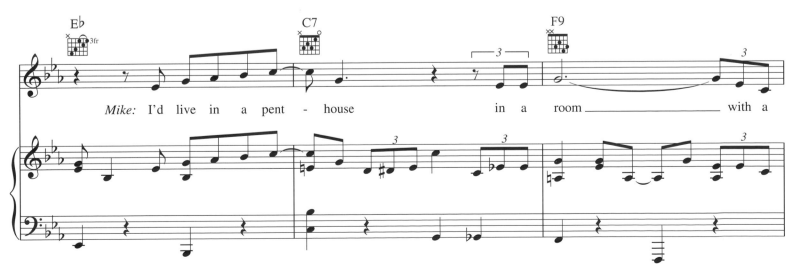

WALK TO WORK

Music by RANDY NEWMAN

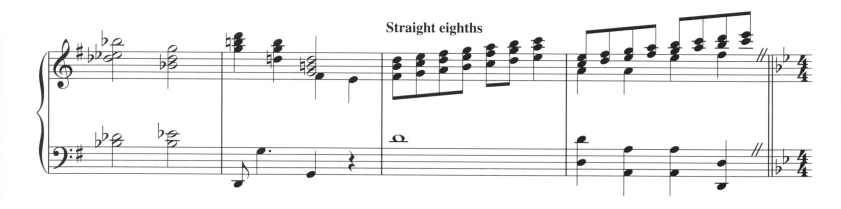

THE SCARE FLOOR

Music by RANDY NEWMAN

Bright Swing

Smoothly

Swing   **D.S. al Coda**

CODA

ENTER THE HEROES

Music by RANDY NEWMAN

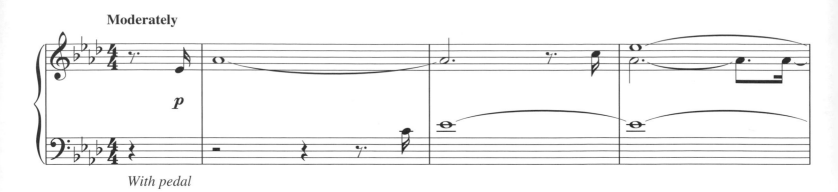

OH, CELIA!

Music by RANDY NEWMAN

Moderate Swing

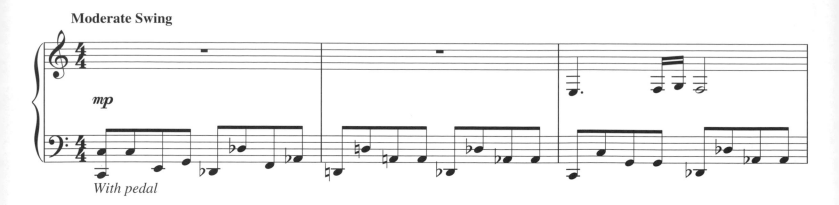

With pedal

BOO'S TIRED

Music by RANDY NEWMAN

YOUNG MICHAEL

Music by Randy Newman

43

FIRST DAY AT MU

Music by RANDY NEWMAN

Bright March tempo

48

SULLEY

Music by RANDY NEWMAN

Slow Swing

mp

With pedal

WASTED POTENTIAL

Music by RANDY NEWMAN

MAIN TITLE
(Monsters University)

Music by RANDY NEWMAN

Fast March tempo

RISE AND SHINE

Music by RANDY NEWMAN

66

GOODBYES

Music by RANDY NEWMAN

68

Very slowly

With more motion

Light Swing

MIKE AND SULLEY

Music by RANDY NEWMAN

March tempo

With pedal

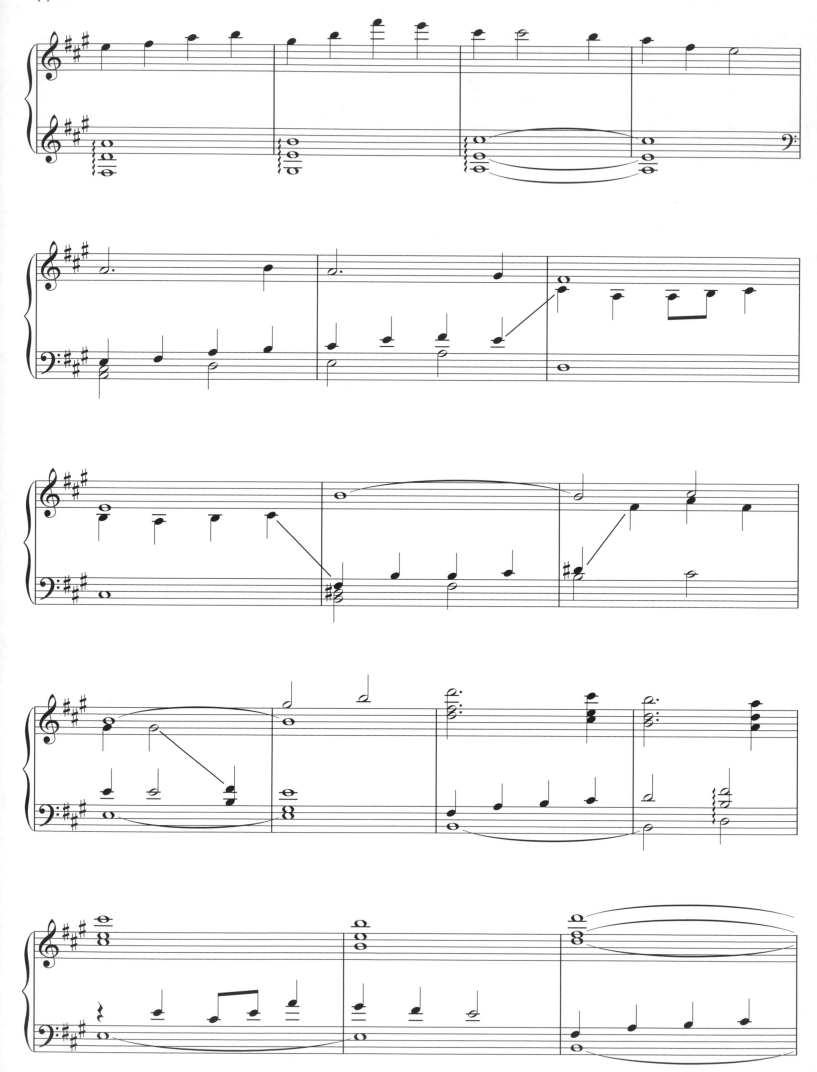

MONSTERS UNIVERSITY

Music by RANDY NEWMAN

Bright March tempo

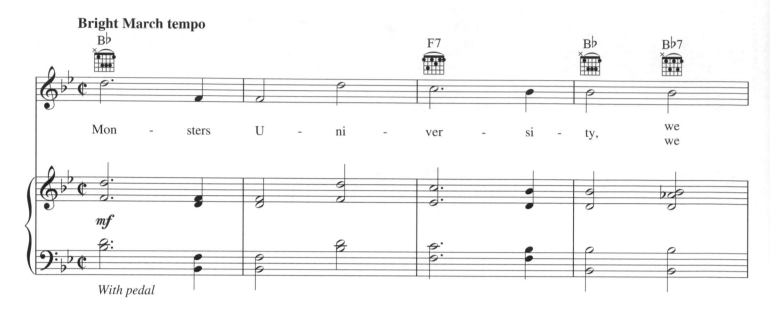

Mon - sters U - ni - ver - si - ty, we
we

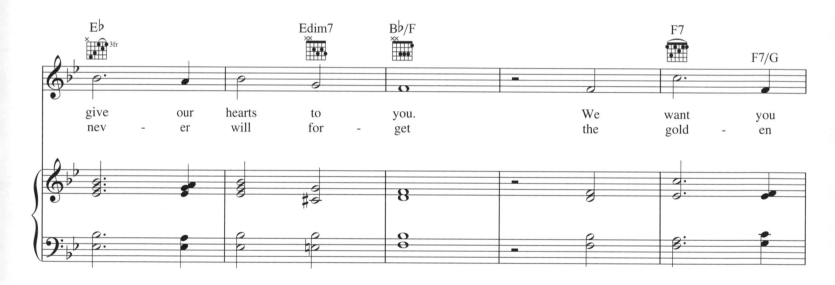

give our hearts to you.
nev - er will for - get

We want you
the gold - en

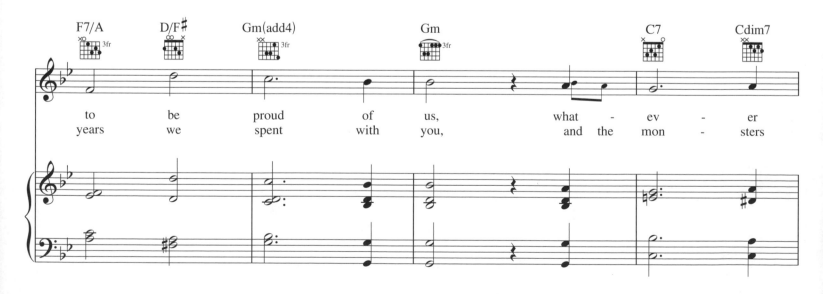

to be proud of us, what - ev - er
years we spent with you, and the mon - sters